Workbook Edition

Author Authority Workbook

How to Write Books That Build Legacy and Launch Movements

Dr. Vernessa Blackwell

Author Authority Workbook: How to Write Books That Build Legacy and Launch Movements

Workbook Edition

Cover Design by **Harien D Layout**

Formatted by **Harien D Layout**

Published by LUI Media

www.lifeuimagined.com

info@lifeuimagined.com

ISBN: 978-1-961743-18-2

Printed in the United States of America

"To every faith-driven visionary—writing, healing, and building legacy one page at a time. May you rise, write, and walk boldly in your Author Authority."

Dr. Vee

Welcome Note

Congratulations on taking this next step—this workbook is your sacred space to apply, reflect, and activate every principle you learned in Author Authority: How to Write Books That Build Legacy and Launch Movements. As you work through each exercise, write boldly, pray deeply, and trust God to guide every stroke of your pen.

Workbook Objectives

1. Clarify your core message and calling.

2. Create actionable plans to write, publish, and brand with purpose.

3. Deepen your faith-driven writing through prayer and reflection.

4. Build confidence in your identity and authority as an author.

5. Lay foundations for your book's impact, marketing, and legacy.

Table of Contents

Chapter 1

You Are the Message

Chapter Summary:

Your story, your scars, and your victories are not random.

You are a living testimony — the message God wants to deliver to others.

Your life is the authority behind the words you are called to write.

Reflection Questions:

1. What experiences in my life have shaped my message?

2. What breakthrough moments could inspire others?

3. What fears have tried to silence my voice?

4. Where have I already seen my story impact others?

5. What parts of my story do I hesitate to share (and why)?

Worksheet / Exercise:

My Message Map

Draw a simple chart:

- In the center: "My Message"
- Surround it with key words/phrases that describe your life experiences, passions, and the legacy you want to leave.

Mini Goal Tracker:

- I completed my Message Map.

- I answered all reflection questions.

Prayer or Affirmation Space:

Affirmation:

I am the living message God is writing through.

Prayer Prompt:

Lord, use my life, my voice, and my testimony to heal, encourage, and lead others into hope.

Notes Page:

Chapter 2

Clarify Your Core Message

Chapter Summary:

Every legacy-driven author must first define their core message.

Your message is the heartbeat of your book, brand, and movement.

Reflection Questions:

1. If I could deliver one message to the world, what would it be?

2. What change do I want my book to create?

3. Who specifically needs to hear my message?

4. What happens if I stay silent?

5. Where do I feel the most passion when speaking or writing?

Worksheet / Exercise:

Message Clarity Exercise:

- **My Core Message in ONE Sentence:** ____________________
- **Who Needs This Message:** ____________________

Mini Goal Tracker:

- **I defined my Core Message.**

- **I identified my audience.**

Prayer or Affirmation Space:

Affirmation:

My message is clear, strong, and necessary.

Prayer Prompt:

Father, help me to articulate the message You placed inside me with clarity and conviction.

Notes Page:

Chapter 3

Own Your Story

Chapter Summary:

Your story holds power when you take ownership of every part — the good, the hard, and the miraculous.

Your authority comes from authenticity.

Reflection Questions:

1. What moments of struggle shaped my strength?

2. How has God redeemed parts of my story?

3. What parts of my story show His glory?

4. What lesson am I uniquely qualified to teach?

5. Where have I already been victorious?

Worksheet / Exercise:

Story Ownership Worksheet:

Write out one defining story from your life and list:

- **The Challenge**
- **The Breakthrough**
- **The Lesson**

Mini Goal Tracker:

- **I wrote my defining story.**

- **I identified the breakthrough.**

Prayer or Affirmation Space:

Affirmation:

I own every part of my story. Nothing is wasted.

Prayer Prompt:

Lord, I thank You for using every chapter of my life for Your glory.

Notes Page:

Chapter 4

Write from a Place of Healing

Chapter Summary:

Healing empowers your writing.

When you write from a place of wholeness, your words carry freedom to others.

Reflection Questions:

1. Am I writing from a healed place or a wounded place?

2. What topics still trigger emotional pain?

3. How can I seek healing before writing on sensitive topics?

4. Who can support my healing journey?

5. What does healed storytelling look like?

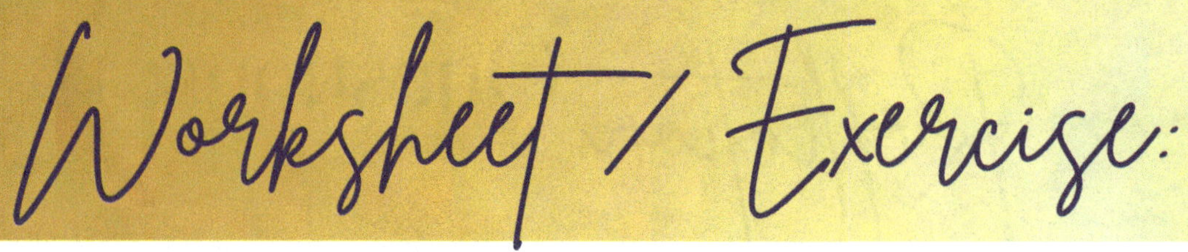

Healing Reflection Sheet:

- **Topics I feel fully healed to write about:** ____________________

- **Topics I need more healing for:** ____________________

Mini Goal Tracker:

- I identified my healing areas.

- I committed to healing before writing sensitive topics.

Prayer or Affirmation Space:

Affirmation:

My healing releases healing to others.

Prayer Prompt:

God, continue to heal the places that will become rivers of living words for others.

Notes Page:

Chapter 5

Build a Movement, Not Just a Book

Chapter Summary:

Your book is the seed — but your calling is to build an ongoing movement.

Think beyond pages. Think legacy.

Reflection Questions:

1. What movement does my book ignite?

2. Who will benefit from this movement?

3. How can I serve beyond the book (events, mentorship, coaching, etc.)?

4. What long-term impact do I dream of creating?

5. What scares me the most about building a movement?

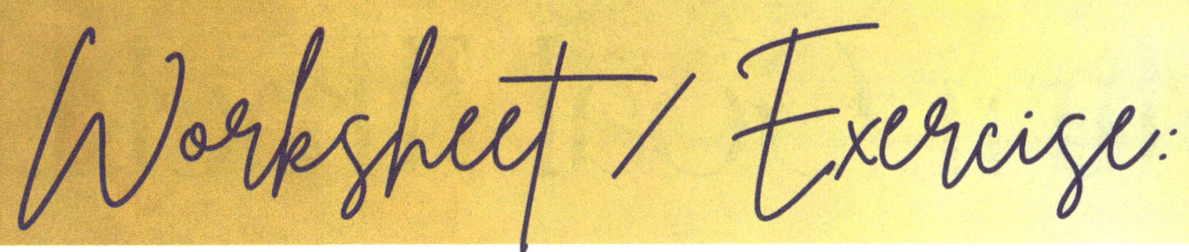

Movement Blueprint:

- **Name of Movement:** ______________________________
- **Mission of Movement:** ____________________________
- **First 3 Actions to Launch:** __________________________

Mini Goal Tracker:

- **I created a Movement Blueprint.**

- **I wrote out my action steps.**

Prayer or Affirmation Space:

Affirmation:

I am building more than a book — I am launching a movement.

Prayer Prompt:

Lord, give me boldness to step into the movement You have assigned to me.

Notes Page:

Chapter 6

Develop Your Author Voice

Chapter Summary:

Your voice is the bridge to your audience.

Authenticity over perfection will always win hearts.

Reflection Questions:

1. How would my best friends describe my natural voice?

2. What tone do I want my writing to carry (e.g., bold, compassionate, empowering)?

3. What fears do I have about showing my true voice?

4. What audience is waiting for my unique sound?

5. How can I write more like I speak?

Worksheet / Exercise:

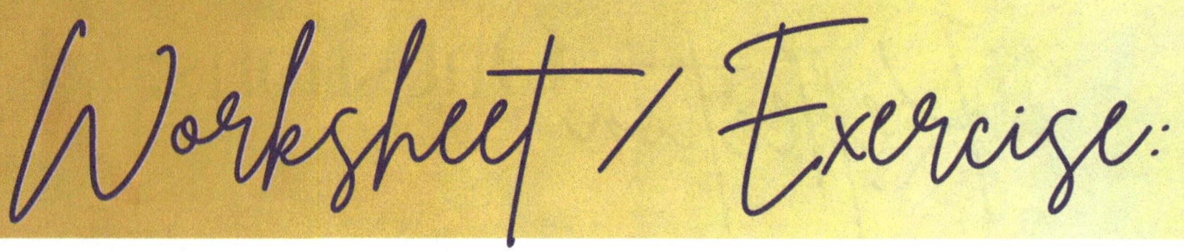

Voice Discovery Exercise:

- **Write a paragraph as if speaking directly to your ideal reader.** ______________________
- **Describe your tone in three words.** ________________

Mini Goal Tracker:

- **I wrote using my natural voice.**

- **I defined my author tone.**

Prayer or Affirmation Space:

Affirmation:

My authentic voice attracts the people I'm called to serve.

Prayer Prompt:

Father, make my voice bold, pure, and aligned with my assignment.

Notes Page:

Chapter 7

Plan to Publish Like a Pro

Chapter Summary:

Publishing professionally means being strategic, prepared, and excellent.

Your message deserves the best presentation.

Reflection Questions:

1. What publishing path is right for me (self-publishing, hybrid, traditional)?

2. What team members will I need (editor, designer, formatter)?

3. What deadlines will keep me accountable?

4. What fears do I have about publishing?

5. How can I honor God with excellence in publishing?

Worksheet / Exercise:

Voice Discovery Exercise:

- **Target Publish Date:** ______________________________
- **Editor/Formatter Contacted:** ______________________
- **Design Ideas/Inspirations:** _______________________

Mini Goal Tracker:

- I created a publishing plan.

- I identified my publishing team needs.

Prayer or Affirmation Space:

Affirmation:

I will publish with excellence and boldness.

Prayer Prompt:

God, surround me with the right people and resources for publishing success.

Notes Page:

Chapter 8

Prepare to Promote Your Message

Chapter Summary:

Promotion is service — not self-centeredness.

You are offering hope, solutions, and transformation.

Reflection Questions:

1. Where will I show up consistently (social media, podcasting, speaking)?

2. What promotional fears must I overcome?

3. How can I lead with value, not salesy pitches?

4. Who can help amplify my message?

5. How will I keep God at the center of my promotion efforts?

Worksheet / Exercise:

Promotion Action Plan:

- **Launch Date:** ____________________
- **3 Platforms I'll focus on:** ____________________
- **5 Value Posts I can create:** ____________________

Mini Goal Tracker:

- I created a promotion plan.

- I posted or practiced sharing my message.

Prayer or Affirmation Space:

Affirmation:

Promotion is part of my obedience, not pride.

Prayer Prompt:

Lord, breathe on every effort to share the message You have entrusted to me.

Notes Page:

Chapter 9

Lead Boldly and Serve Faithfully

Chapter Summary:

Authority is leadership, and leadership is service.

Step into your role as a servant-leader through authorship.

Reflection Questions:

1. What does servant leadership mean to me?

2. How will I lead with humility and courage?

3. What legacy am I building beyond my book?

4. Who can I mentor and empower?

5. What prayers will sustain my leadership?

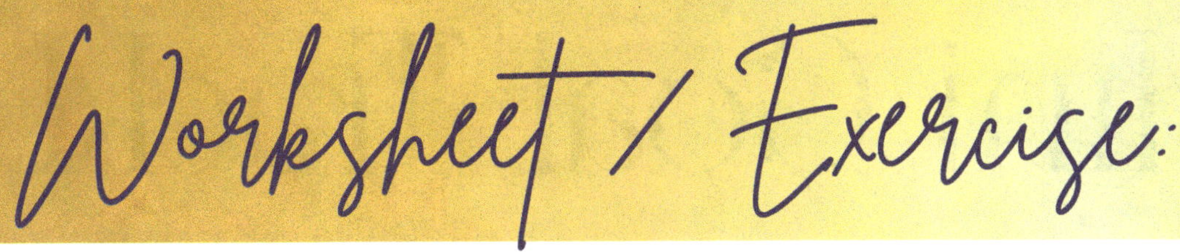

Leadership Vision Sheet:

- **My Leadership Style:** ______________________________
- **My Leadership Mission:** ______________________________

Mini Goal Tracker:

- I created my leadership mission.

- I identified one person I can mentor.

Prayer or Affirmation Space:

Affirmation:

I lead with faith, courage, and humility.

Prayer Prompt:

Father, lead me as I lead others.

Notes Page:

Chapter 10

Legacy Over Limelight

Chapter Summary:

Your goal is legacy, not likes.

Focus on what will matter 10, 20, 100 years from now.

Reflection Questions:

1. What legacy do I want my writing to leave?

2. What values must I live by consistently?

3. Who am I writing for beyond this generation?

4. What would I want future readers to say about my work?

5. What is one small step I can take today to secure my legacy?

Worksheet / Exercise:

Legacy Builder Sheet:

- **5 Words I want associated with my name:** ________
- **Final Message to Future Generations:** ___________

Mini Goal Tracker:

- I wrote my legacy goals.

- I reflected on long-term impact.

Prayer or Affirmation Space:

Affirmation:

I am called to build legacy, not chase limelight.

Prayer Prompt:

Lord, let my life and words echo beyond my lifetime.

Notes Page:

Your Author Mindset

Author Mindset Checklist:

- **I believe that my voice matters and has the power to change lives.**
- **I choose to release any fears or doubts about my writing journey.**
- **I embrace my calling as an author and recognize that it is part of my purpose.**
- **I commit to staying consistent and disciplined with my writing.**
- **I trust in God's timing for my book and the impact it will make.**

Reflection Questions:

1. **What mindset shift do I need to make to move forward confidently in my writing?**

2. What limiting beliefs must I let go of to write with freedom?

Affirmation:

I am a confident, purposeful author, walking in the fullness of my calling.

Bonus Page 2: Time Management for Authors

Block Out Writing Time:

1. Block Out Writing Time:

Schedule daily or weekly writing blocks to stay on track. Treat your writing time as a non-negotiable appointment.

2. Set Realistic Goals:

Focus on writing achievable daily or weekly word counts. Don't aim for perfection, just progress.

3. Remove Distractions:

Minimize distractions during your writing time (e.g., turn off notifications, clear your workspace).

4. Use a Timer:

Set a timer for short writing sprints (e.g., 25 minutes). This method encourages focus and productivity.

5. Delegate Tasks:

If possible, outsource or delegate non-writing tasks to free up more time for writing.

Reflection Exercise:

What are the biggest distractions in my writing process, and how can I eliminate them?

Bonus Page 3: Building Your Author Brand

Key Elements of an Author Brand:

1. Clear Vision and Mission:

Define what your brand stands for and the values you wish to represent through your writing.

2. Visual Identity:

Consider colors, logos, and fonts that reflect your book's themes and your personal style.

3. Online Presence:

Create and maintain active social media profiles, a website, and possibly a blog to stay connected with readers.

4. Consistency:

Keep your messaging and content consistent across all platforms. Be authentic and true to your brand.

5. Engagement:

Engage with your audience through social media posts, newsletters, and other interactive content.

Action Steps:

- **My Author Brand Vision:**

- **What Visuals Represent My Brand:**

Bonus Page 4: Creating a Legacy

Legacy Building Tips:

1. Write with the Next Generation in Mind:

When writing, think of the impact your work will have on future generations. Your words carry the potential for lasting influence.

2. Serve and Empower Others:

Use your platform to inspire, educate, and empower others to reach their potential.

3. Leave Behind More Than Just a Book:

Build resources such as courses, coaching programs, or other educational content that will continue your legacy.

4. Invest in Mentorship:

One of the greatest ways to build a legacy is by mentoring others and helping them realize their own dreams.

Reflect and Action:

- **What legacy do I want to leave through my writing?**

- **How can I start building that legacy today?**

Bonus Page 5: Your Author Action Plan

Action Plan:

1. Define Your Goal:

What is your main goal for your book? (e.g., impact, reach, sales, etc.)

2. Set Milestones:

Break down your goal into achievable milestones. This could include timelines for completing drafts, editing, and marketing.

3. Create Accountability:

Who will you share your progress with, and how will they hold you accountable?

4. Celebrate Your Wins:

How will you celebrate your progress?

Bonus Page 6: Prayer Journal for Authors

Opening Prayer for Writing:

Lord, thank You for the opportunity to write and share my message with the world. I pray for Your guidance and wisdom as I write that my words will bring hope, healing, and transformation to those who read them. Help me to stay focused, disciplined, and true to the message You have entrusted to me.

Daily Prayer Journal Prompts:

- Today, I pray for clarity in my writing.
- Lord, help me to overcome any doubts or fears.
- I pray for peace and focus as I continue to write.
- God, I thank You for the inspiration that fills my heart and the creativity You've blessed me with.

Bonus Page 7: Resources & Tools for Authors

Recommended Resources:

1. **Book Writing Software:**
   - **Scrivener: Great for organizing your manuscript.**
   - **Google Docs: Easy collaboration and accessibility.**

2. **Editing Tools:**
   - **ProWritingAid: An excellent editing tool to polish your writing.**
   - **Grammarly: Helps catch grammar errors and improve readability.**

3. **Cover Design & Formatting:**
   - **Canva: Easy-to-use design tool for covers and marketing materials.**
   - **Reedsy: Offers professional book formatting services.**

4. **Self-Publishing Platforms:**
   - **Amazon KDP: Great for self-publishing your book.**
   - **IngramSpark: Ideal for print-on-demand and distribution to bookstores**

Final Thoughts:

Writing a book is a journey of dedication, faith, and courage. As you move through each step, always keep your eyes on the impact you are creating and the legacy you are building. You are not just writing a book — you are making a lasting difference in the world.

Now go and write your legacy

"Building Legacy, One Word at a Time."

Certificate of Completion

Certificate of Completion ______________________

This is to certify that

[Recipient's Name]

Has successfully completed the

Author Authority Workbook

How to Write Books That Build Legacy and Launch Movements

Date of Completion:

Instructor/Coach: Dr. Vernessa Blackwell

This certificate is awarded in recognition of the recipient's dedication to building their author legacy and launching a movement through writing.

Signature:

Dr. Vernessa Blackwell

Founder & Author Strategist

Vermaro Christian University

Made in the USA
Monee, IL
21 August 2025